Austerity Ulster 1947-51

Photos from the UTA Archive 1

NORMAN JOHNSTON

Austerity Ulster 1947-1951

Norman Johnston is a native of Northern Ireland and a retired teacher. He has written several history textbooks for schools and has always had an interest in transport. He is the author of many books on transport subjects ranging from *The Fintona Horse Tram* to *Locomotives of the GNRI*. Since retiring he has become a publisher and was a founder of Colourpoint Books.

First Impression

Designed by Colourpoint Books, Newtownards
Printed by: GPS Colour Graphics Ltd

ISBN 978 1 904242 89 5

Colourpoint Books
Colourpoint House
Jubilee Business Park
21 Jubilee Road
Newtownards
County Down
Northern Ireland
BT23 4YH
Tel: 028 9182 0505
Fax: 028 9182 1900
E-mail: info@colourpoint.co.uk
Web-site: www.colourpoint.co.uk

Cover photographs

Front cover: This rural scene, on 15 September 1951, encapsulates much of the character of Northern Ireland in the early post-war years. The occasion is the Dundrod Races of 1951 and spectators are arriving by bus to watch the event. Members of the RUC are on hand to direct traffic and a typical Ulster farmhouse forms the backdrop.

Rear cover

Left: Mogul No 100 *Queen Elizabeth* at Antrim with the Festival train on 28 April 1951.

Right: A UTA bus Inspector briefs a conductor and driver on their next duties at North Street yard, Belfast, on 6 September 1951.

Introduction

Austerity Ulster 1947-1951

The origins of this book go back to the discovery of an old photo album in a loft after someone made a house move in 2006. The album turned out to be a collection of official photographs taken by, or for, the Ulster Transport Authority in the years 1947 to 1959 and has been acquired by Colourpoint. The pictures record the activities and interests of the UTA in this period.

For younger readers, who may never have heard of the UTA, I should explain that the UTA was a forerunner of today's Translink, the state-owned concern which integrates the activities of Ulsterbus, Metro and Northern Ireland Railways. However, away back in the 1930s and earlier, public transport was operated by independent bus, train and lorry operators.

In 1935 the Northern Ireland government established the Northern Ireland Road Transport Board (NIRTB) which took over all the private bus and lorry operators in the province and was given a monopoly of all public transport by road – effectively nationalisation of road transport. The only exception to the monopoly (other than companies operating on both sides of the border) was Belfast, where the Corporation operated their own buses, the successor to which is now Citybus or Metro. Within the city, Belfast Corporation had a monopoly and the NIRTB could drop, but not pick up, fare-paying passengers on their way into the city and could pick up, but not drop, on out-bound services.The NIRTB buses operated from Smithfield bus station, as depicted in this book.

At first, the railways continued to be independent, with the NIRTB competing against them. However, in 1948, as the financial state of the railways worsened, it was decided to combine the Northern Counties Committee railway (NCC, York Road towards Larne, Portrush and Londonderry), the Belfast and County Down Railway (BCDR, Queens Quay towards Bangor, Donaghadee and Newcastle) with the NIRTB to create the UTA. The UTA now controlled all public transport operating entirely within the province – trains, buses and lorries – apart from Belfast Corporation. The various cross-border railways and road transport companies were excluded from the take over as they were partly in the Republic of Ireland. The largest of these was the Great Northern Railway (Great Victoria Street towards Dublin, Omagh, Derry, Enniskillen, Newry, Clones, etc). The UTA also controlled the former railway hotels such as the *Slieve Donard*, Newcastle, the *Northern Counties*, Portrush and the *Laharna*, Larne.

Thus from 1948 to about 1967 the Ulster Transport Authority, with its green trains and road vehicles, was synonymous with transport for everyone who lived in Northern Ireland in that era. The UTA not only had a monopoly but had also an *obligation* to provide transport (at strictly regulated rates) for any goods the public cared to offer it. Thus even if the transport of 200 eggs from a farm in Ahoghill to Ballymena could only be done at a loss by the UTA, it still had to take them!

There were still private operators lorries on the roads, but they were only allowed to transport *their own* goods. For example Dowlers of Lisnaskea, Co Fermanagh, had several lorries used to collect goods from the docks for sale in their shop and for delivery to customers, but could not use their vans or lorries for transporting on behalf of someone else.

In 1964 it was decided to break up the UTA monopoly and in particular to privatise freight. Most internal rail freight ended at the beginning of 1965. Later in that year the road freight division became Northern Ireland Carriers (NIC) using a red livery, but had to compete with any private road operators who entered the field. It was later absorbed by the National Freight Corporation, and has now disappeared. The railway side became NIR in 1967 and today is an exclusively passenger operator. The buses became Ulsterbus in 1967 and in theory private operators could take over groups of services to compete. In practice only two were created – Coastal Bus Service (Portrush) and Sureline (Lurgan), both now long gone.

For me personally, the discovery of this UTA album brought back many memories, as I grew up in a UTA family. My father worked at Portadown on the road freight side of the UTA empire, not as a lorry driver but as one of the army of UTA clerks who processed all the waybills and consignment notes that the system generated.

This is the first of three books based on the album and concentrates on the period when the UTA was being established. It reflects an era that coincides with my early childhood and as I look at the pictures memories flood back of the way people dressed in those years of austerity, when wages were low and there were widespread shortages. Many of the cars seen on the road were prewar models with running boards and upright side valve engines. Black was the prevailing colour.

The album itself seems to have been started by the NIRTB in May 1947 and initially concentrates on bus and lorry subjects. However, after the takeover of the BCDR and NCC in 1948, the album begins to reflect the newly acquired train and hotel interests of the UTA. Gradually the scope of the album widens to include not only new vehicles and rolling stock but a record of everyday operations – conductors on rural buses delivering parcels, a train guard waving his green flag, street scenes outside UTA buildings and eventually assignments to photograph local tourist attractions, no doubt to acquire pictures for leaflets promoting UTA leisure travel.

There is also a major section recording the construction of the huge UTA joint road/rail engineering works at Duncrue Street, still partly used by Ulsterbus. This coverage starts with the clearing of the site from August 1948 and ends with its opening in 1950.

I was particularly delighted to find lots of pictures of what we called the 'wee bus', a one sixth scale model of a UTA double-decker. This vehicle was immensely popular and would appear at the UTA stand at the Balmoral Show, giving rides to children if appropriate. At Christmas it did the rounds of the UTA parties and as a small child I remember it inside Portadown Town Hall, bringing the children of UTA employees up to the front of the hall to collect their presents from Santa. It started off in 1947 in NIRTB livery but soon got the current UTA version (which reversed the two shades of green) and in 1968 was eventually painted into Ulsterbus blue and white. When Ulsterbus withdrew their last half-cab double-decker, the 'wee bus' was donated to the Transport Museum.

So enjoy this rather unusual transport album and, as you leaf through it, if you are a younger reader, you will get some insight into life at a time when 'baby-boomers' like myself were in their childhood. Far gone is the time when crowds of people would line the street to watch a procession of commercial vehicles and buses in the Lord Mayor's Show or when going on holiday meant heading for Portrush and arriving by bus or taxi at York Road station with loads of luggage and two railway porters to carry it!

Balmoral Show

Our coverage begins with a look at the transport stand at the Balmoral Show, which in May 1947 was just outside the New Harberton Hall. The NIRTB was represented by three vehicles. On the right is one of the new Leyland PS1 single deckers then being constructed in the body shop at Dunmurry, whilst on the left is a new PD1A double decker with a standard Leyland body, No A911 (GZ 4729) for those interested.

In the background is a small Scammell MH mechanical horse (X3031) attached to a box trailer. The 'X' prefix dates it to 1944, just as the 'A' prefix on the bus indicates a 1947 vehicle. The Board and the UTA used a different letter for each year starting with 'A' for 1923. Having reached 'Z' in 1946, they started over again the following year. The letters 'I' and 'O' were not used.

As mentioned in the introduction, the poster in the foreground draws attention to the 'door to door' nature of NIRTB freight services. Note the abbreviated form of 'Road Transport Board'.

A year later it was showtime again and the outdoor exhibits were in exactly the same spot. In May 1948 it was still the Board as the UTA did not officially take over until October.

As was only natural, the NIRTB displayed its latest vehicles to the public and in 1948 it had to be the new 'half-decker' that had just emerged from Dunmurry on a Leyland PS2/10 chassis. This was the first of six intended for the Enniskillen and Omagh long distance services.

The door at the back, which the crowd is investigating, is not the passenger door but the entry to the large luggage compartment. Up to then standard buses on this route often had 10 of the 34 seats occupied by luggage and parcels.

Although not visible because of the throng, the bus had two front steering axles which allowed it to exceed the legal 27'6" limit for two axle vehicles. Unfortunately the Ministry of Home Affairs, who were the PSV authority, refused to clear a 30'0" vehicle for these routes, which was not helpful. The NIRTB had already taken delivery of a second chassis but managed to cancel the final four. The UTA bodied the second chassis in 1951 and used the two half-deckers on the Nutts Corner airport service.

One of the big crowd pullers at the 1948 Balmoral Show was the large model railway inside the King's Hall. This was part of the indoor section of the NIRTB display. Note the number of young boys in this predominantly male audience.

Electric model railways were virtually unobtainable in 1948 due to the emphasis on exports and, as they were the most sophisticated mechanical toys on the market, every schoolboy wanted one. The model buses and lorries in the foreground were also powered, with an early form of Scalectric and include a model of the half-decker depicted opposite. The trains seem to be NCC based.

In the background are display stands for JHA Swinson & Co of York Street and GEC Electrics.

Visible in the background of the previous picture was part of the information desk at the NIRTB stand. The backdrops gave a representation of what the view from a bus window might be like and bus seats have been placed below them.

Two rather self conscious Board secretaries have the role of handing out leaflets and selling bus timetables. They are typical 1948 beauties with something of the Rita Hayworth look.

The ladies in the background are dressed in typical ladies' fashions of the late forties, costume suits and even hats being common on an Ulster 'day out'.

At the May 1948 Balmoral Show the 'wee bus' had also made its appearance. Just completed at the NIRTB workshops, it had an electric motor and was a fair representation of a Leyland PD1. It was given the fictitious fleet number C969 and registration MZ 1948 (reflecting the year). To accommodate passengers, it was not double deck inside. The little conductor was the son of an NIRTB senior manager. The bus did a circuit round the King's Hall, stopping at the main entrance.

By 1949 the 'wee bus' had been repainted into UTA livery. The dark colour was Brunswick green and the lighter colour something akin to a 'Granny Smith' apple. The NIRTB had used the same two shades in reverse. The bus no doubt caused some bystanders in East Bridge Street to wipe their glasses as it passed on the back of a UTA flat-bed lorry at the Industrial and Military Parade on Saturday 22 October 1949, during Belfast Saving's Week. Ahead of the lorry is a standard NIRTB-bodied Leyland PS1 single decker. Note the tram tracks and square setts and the wires for both trams and trolleybuses. The tower of Chichester Street fire station can be seen on the right.

By 1951 the UTA was well established and this interesting view was taken at the Balmoral Show 23-26 May that year. The UTA stand is viewed from the balcony of the King's Hall, looking towards the Lisburn Road giving a panorama of quite a selection of the indoor stands. The 'wee bus' features again, but has been re-registered OZ 1951 (MZ 1948 was now used by a 1949 PS2 single decker). On the UTA stand itself, notice how the different facets of the Authority are reflected in the advertising. Note the stand on the right for the recently formed British European Airways (BEA).

Another view of the UTA display at the 1951 Balmoral Show, staffed this time by two fairly prim ladies in suits, though perhaps the seated lady is a customer. The 'wee bus' is now a static exhibit. The hotels featured in the display are the Midland (Belfast), Slieve Donard (Newcastle) and Northern Counties (Portrush). The bus photographs feature the latest front entrance single deckers, the first of which appeared in 1951. Few office workers, familiar with modern photocopiers, will have worked with the large fluid-based duplicators displayed on the Roneo stand in the left background. These used messy ink 'masters' and left the operator needing defumigated! However, they were 'state of the art' in 1951.

Smithfield Bus Station

Few people under the age of forty will remember Smithfield Bus Station, which disappeared from the scene in 1978. This 1947 view shows the Winetavern Street entrance looking towards North Street, which is marked by the tall houses in the background. Buses entering the depot went through one of the two entrances to 'The Pens' to pick up passengers. They then left 'The Shed', as it was called, by an exit at the far end of the building. Just over the wall on the left are buses parked on the site of a former factory.

This is a later view of Smithfield Bus Depot, on 29 April 1951, viewed from West Street, which ran between Winetavern Street (to the right) and Millfield. The ladies heading into town are in typical early 1950s clothes. By 1951 the bus park referred to on page 13 had been opened up to create the new bus stands seen on the left. 'The shed' was at right angles to these and its roof can be seen behind the distant bus. Three different types of double-decker are in view, including one of the recent 1950 Leyland PD2/1s on the right and a 1936 Leyland TD4 on the left. Buses entered this part of the bus station by going through a new entrance from Winetavern Street, out of view to the right.

A rare view inside 'The Shed' on 1 September 1951. The single deck buses are both Leyland, a PS1 on the left and a PS2 on the right (note the different styles of rear window.

Passengers stood on raised platforms in 'The Pens' and close examination of the photo shows all the typical types present – businessmen, shoppers, workers heading home, bored children asking "Is this ours now, Mummy?", schoolboys, etc.

'The Pens' got their nickname because of their resemblance to those used at cattle marts.

The No 105 bus is heading for Crumlin and the No 61 for Enniskillen, via Armagh. In later years, as Smithfield became more congested, both these routes and many others were moved to new departure points at College Square East.

Shortly after taking over the railways, the official photographer was given the job of recording the UTA's new railway assets and this is one of his views of the former BCDR terminus at Queen's Quay on 12 November 1948. We are looking towards the confectionery and fruit shop on the concourse between platforms 4 and 5, seemingly encouraging patriotic eating. The advertisement above Platform 4 asks "Did you MACLEAN your teeth today?" On the left is a weighing scale, as most railways seemed to cater for passengers who had an irresistible urge to find out if they were still 12 stone or now 14.

Three years later, the UTA photographer was back at Queen's Quay Station, recording some everyday scenes of steam trains departing. This one, on 7 September 1951, reminds us of long forgotten aspects of railway operation. The guard stands in his van while a passenger discusses some issue relating to his luggage. The trolley with luggage and parcels, and even the porter in attendance, no longer feature on railways, which today have few long distance passengers with luggage. The train is heading for Bangor, the only destination from Queens Quay after the closure of the rest of the BCDR system early in 1950. Most suburban steam trains in the 1950s comprised non-corridor compartment stock with slam doors, these examples being ex-NCC stock built in the 1930s.

272

York Road Station

Opposite: Another tradition which is now a thing of the past was the guard waving the green flag and blowing his whistle to indicate to the engine driver that he was ready to depart. Today the train conductor simply uses a bell which rings in the cab of the diesel railcar.

On 7 September 1951 the guard performs the age old ritual with the 11.15 to Bangor.

Right: Two young women cross Whitla Street towards York Road Station on 29 April 1951. This was the former LMS (NCC) terminus and was one of the few stations in the UK where trains entered the station building (another was Queen's Quay). The tram canopy can be seen on the right and was removed six months after this picture was taken.

A view inside the tram canopy at York Road Station on Wednesday 1 December 1948. The canopy was used by taxis and delivery vans as well as trams. The canopy gave direct access to the concourse and platforms and Platform 3 is visible in the background.

The taxi in the foreground is an Austin 16/18, a model in production from 1935 to 1937. These spacious cars seated six in the back in facing seats. Note that it has a disc wheel on the rear, as opposed to the more normal wire at the front. Just visible behind is a Ford Eight. I wonder how many people can remember the Borough Building Society, advertised above the taxi. Note the promotion for the King George's Fund for Sailors.

York Road station had been remodelled in 1894 by Berkley Dean Wise when he added the tram canopy opposite. He also introduced some Swiss style features such as the sales kiosks for confectionery, tobacco and books, seen here on 1 December 1948. This feature is now preserved at the railway gallery in the Ulster Folk and Transport Museum, where it is the Midland Buffet. The war memorial, erected in 1920, is partly obscured by the pillar.

In 1948 the Radio Times was just that, at least as far as Northern Ireland was concerned. TV did not arrive until 1953. Below the advertisement is the gate through to Platform 1.

A busy scene at York Road Station on a damp Friday 24 August 1951. The two cars are Vauxhalls, that in the foreground being a 1937 'Big Six' BXL which had a 3180cc OHV engine. Just arrived at Platform 4 is one of the NCC WT class 2-6-4Ts, suggesting that this is probably the morning boat train from Larne. It is an atmospheric scene of bustle and activity as passengers scramble for taxis and buses to take them to their final destinations. Gabardine coats predominate.

This view was taken on the same occasion but looking towards the ticket barrier as passengers from Stranraer make their way out onto the concourse. Platform 5 had been shortened to create the taxi rank and the ladies are standing on what was once the platform edge. Two trolleys are in view and the front one is probably in use for a passenger with a lot of luggage, perhaps the middle aged lady in the background. The porter nearest the camera has what appear to be baskets of salt or iced fish in tow. Today's traveller would be hard put to find help with luggage at a modern station!

The following Saturday, 1 September 1951, the photographer was back in York Road to photograph the procedure of buying train tickets. The ticket office was another of Berkley Dean Wise's chalet-style buildings and the passengers include soldiers with their kit bags heading off to rejoin their regiments in England, possibly to fight in the Korean War.

Large parcels tied with string were much easier to carry than today's sellotaped variety.

On the same occasion we have an interesting close up of an elderly gentleman buying a ticket. Tickets were of the Edmondson card type in those days and were preprinted. The glass partition with small opening reflected the need for security to prevent theft and the perforated speaking grill avoided confusion between Ballymena and Ballymoney or between Kerry and Derry! The layout is reminiscent of contemporary banks.

At this time, and indeed well into the sixties, most men dressed fairly conservatively with suit, tie, overcoat and hat.

Viewed from inside, we see the same scene from the perspective of the ticket clerk. The racks of Edmondson tickets can be seen on the right, with more out of view to the left; notice the cash drawer open in the foreground.

The ticket stock would all be pre-printed for journeys commencing at Belfast (York Road). These would be for every conceivable destination, from common ones like Antrim and Larne to more obscure ones like Carrichue and Killagan, not to mention destinations in England or on other Irish systems. For each destination there were then variations like Return and Single and first or second class. There were of course blanks with just 'Belfast YR to . . ." which were filled in – Grayrigg, St Austell or wherever.

Here the clerk is possibly dealing with a travel warrant for a military officer. Details of the warrant had to be recorded so that the ticket cost could be reclaimed from the Ministry of Defence. The soldier retained the warrant for other parts of his journey.

Railway operation in the 1950s and 1960s was very labour intensive and major stations had an army of porters, not merely for assisting passengers but for loading parcels and mail. Here, on 24 October 1951, porters are busy loading mail into a 'V' van at Platform 2, York Road, the train being the 10.55am to Londonderry. A 'V' van was a full brake bogie van which carried only luggage and the guard. It had six sets of double doors to speed loading and unloading.

Bangor

Moving away from Belfast, we have a front aspect of Bangor railway station on 3 February 1948 with three fairly new NIRTB buses parked outside. Thankfully the photograph predates the 'modernisation' by the UTA in 1950 when the attractive brick Italianate building, designed by Sir Charles Lanyon, was plastered over and the arched windows squared off. The stationmaster's house is also still there, on the site of the present bus station. Several cars are in view, that nearer the camera being a new Hillman Minx and the more distant one a Morris Eight. The large advertisement beside the clock is for Ormo bread while the clock tower promotes Denny's bacon and sausages.

Poster sites at Bangor Pier on 7 July 1951. This is a picture that really brings me back, as my interest in old cars was sparked off by seeing pre-war cars parked along Bangor seafront, as in the background here. Also in the background are the coastguard station (since replaced and now a restaurant) the castle, the Marine Court Hotel and the Royal Hotel. Coach tours are on offer to the Mournes, Warrenpoint, and more distant places like Dublin, Bundoran and Rossapenna. The other display will evoke memories for those old enough to recall the Clifton and Captain ballrooms, Fred Perry and Dan Maskell playing tennis at Bangor and plays like *The Chiltern Hundreds* in the Guild Theatre.

In the 1940s and 1950s the newly formed British Railways ran a travel office in Belfast, in cooperation with the UTA. In those days there were few travel agents and BR were primarily promoting their shipping services and onward connections to London, Edinburgh, etc. The office was No 24 Donegall Place on the corner of Castle Lane, and is now a jewellers. This view, on 15 April 1949, reminds us that the horse-drawn era was still with us, as evidenced by the milk cart. Square sets and tram tracks occupy the centre part of most streets. Note the old-fashioned 'No entry' sign on Castle Lane.

Management of both road and rail transport after 1948, with considerable forwarding of consignments by road from railhead, soon focused the minds of the UTA on how road/rail interchange could be achieved. The traditional method was wasteful loading and unloading by hand or crane. One solution explored by the UTA was an articulated lorry trailer which could be reversed onto a bogie well wagon. A special motorised, but hand-steered, hydraulic truck was then used to swing the trailer through 90 degrees to align it with the wagon. The official photographer was on hand at York Road on 9 February 1949 to record a trial. The main problem was that loading was still time consuming and required too much skill on the part of the lorry driver and shunter to position it correctly. Imagine loading twenty of these! It would probably have taken six hours.

We now have two interior views of a brand new double deck bus at Dunmurry on 11 February 1949.

Because some main roads were crossed by low railway bridges, all double deckers had to be of the 'low bridge' type with a low overall height to get under them.

To reduce the height, the aisle of the upper deck was aligned to the offside and protruded into the downstairs deck, as we can see. How many readers remember banging their head if they stood up suddenly from the right hand seats? There were warning notices about this on the backs of the right hand seats.

Note the art deco style interior lights used by the NIRTB and UTA. A small sliding window at the rear of the cab allowed the driver to communicate with the conductor.

The upstairs view is looking towards the rear. The aisle is on the left and all the seats bench ones that you had to step up into. Inevitably, if you sat on the nearside, alighting required getting past other passengers but the legroom was generous and this was not too difficult.

The mirror marks the top of the stairs. Note that the rear window frame hinged downwards to serves as the emergency door.

The window ventilators were of the sliding type, as on modern trains of the period, but older buses often had the winding type.

The bus used for these pictures was No B863 (MZ 304), a Leyland PD1A, which, although completed in early 1949, appeared in the NIRTB version of the livery with the light green dominant.

Duncrue Street Works

One of the first things the UTA did was to build a new combined road/rail engineering works at Duncrue Street to replace the Dunmurry body-building plant and other facilities at University Street. These two pictures were taken on Monday 18 July 1949 not long after it opened. We are looking towards Milewater Road in this picture and at this early stage there is not too much clutter. In the distance buses are under repair with lorries also in view and workbenches in the foreground. The boxes at the bottom are marked 'Electrical Dep, Rolling Stock'.

The second view is from the same position but looking towards the left. The general impression is of a spacious facility but one which still depended on a lot of labour-intensive work. These benches have lathes, jigs, drilling machinery and saws for machining and fitting parts. By modern standards this would be a very expensive facility to operate but in the late 1940s industrial wages were still very low. Note the container marked with a red cross, probably a first aid store. The trucks appear to be flatbed Albions.

This is a later shot of Duncrue Street Works taken on Monday 28 August 1950. I have included this view as it is looking in the opposite direction to the previous ones, towards the railway side of the facility.

The carriages under construction here are for the new 'Festival Express' that was planned for the following year (see pages 52–54). To the right, goods vans are under repair.

Also visible are five standard Leyland PS1 single deckers, of which the UTA had over 400. In the foreground is a rather ancient 'forward control' Leyland Beaver cattle truck (fleet number 3305), dating probably from 1936. Beyond the bus on the right is a Commer Q4 parcel delivery van and a Bedford MLD flat-bed lorry.

Meet the photographer and his assistant . . .! This view was taken on the Malone Road on 22 March 1951 as the photographer's equipment was either loaded or unloaded. His roomy car is one of the superb Vauxhall J series introduced in 1938, over 30,000 of which were produced post-war. They had a 1781cc six cylinder engine and a roomy interior and this view gives a glimpse of the door trim and dash.

The UTA property portfolio included the famous Northern Counties Hotel, Portrush, seen in August 1949. This hotel no longer exists following a disastrous fire in the 1980s. As the name suggests, this prestige hotel was built by the Belfast and Northern Counties Railway, later LMS(NCC), and was acquired by the UTA when it took over the NCC in 1949. In the 1930s it was the place to be seen for the rich and famous. Sadly, the development of continental holidays in the 1960s destroyed its raison d'être.

Another well-known railway hotel in the UTA family was the Midland Hotel, beside York Road Station and built by the BNCR in 1898. It was renamed after the Midland Railway bought the BNCR in 1903.

This view was taken on 17 August 1951 looking along Whitla Street towards the tram bay at the station, demolished soon after.

The hotel was bombed during the 1941 Blitz and its post-war rebuilding resulted in more austere lines than the high Victorian Northern Counties.

A variety of cars are parked on the street, from left to right a new Austin Hereford, a 1937 Vauxhall 'Big Six', a 1949 Standard Vanguard Phase I, a 1948 Vauxhall J type and a new Vauxhall L type Velox. On the extreme right is a 1948 Hillman Minx Phase III.

Heavy haulage was a UTA speciality and because it had a monopoly of transport it had equipment to meet every requirement, however challenging.

Few can have been more challenging than the delivery of this industrial boiler from Daniel Adamson & Co Ltd, Dukinfield, to Messrs Frazer & Haughton Ltd of Cullybackey on 23 October 1949.

To start with, the Scammell lorry and trailer had to negotiate a narrow entrance road with various twists and turns around buildings to get to where we see it here. The final destination of the boiler was this building and it had to pass through the right hand archway.

The UTA staff are attempting to line up the trailer with the archway and from other photographs the clearance was about six inches (150mm) all round! What appear at first glance to be cracks in the negative are in fact cables running from the building on the right, just another little something to complicate the job.

In the second view, the trailer has been straightened to align with the building, but it still needs to be lowered and pushed a few feet more to the right. Later the boiler was jacked up with baulks and the trailer removed. It was then gradually pushed in using timbers and jacks.

Just after the Second World War, the NIRTB had acquired an ex-Ministry of Aircraft Production factory at Dunmurry, used to make sea rescue equipment. They converted it into a new Body Building Shop and opened it in April 1946. It continued to be used by the UTA until 1952, well after Duncrue Street was up and running. This view shows the exterior of the shop on 1 March 1950. The bus is a 1936 AEC Regal with EEC body, No P189 (EZ 1760). Originally diesel-engined, it was given a petrol engine in 1951 and survived until 1955.

Although Dunmurry's primary function was building buses, they also constructed a batch of 'brown vans' for the NCC section of the railway in 1949. In addition one carriage was built at Dunmurry, dining car No 87 and this picture shows the heavy haulage department transporting it to York Road Station on 5 March 1950. The trailer being used here was the same one seen earlier at Cullybackey and was known as the 'Jerry truck'. Originally a Panzer transporter, it had come to Northern Ireland about 1946 as part of German reparations. It was a versatile vehicle as the six axles could be in three sets of two or two sets of three, depending on the length of the load. McCreary tram No 459 and Chamberlain No 341 appear in this view of Donegall Place as the load passes Austin Reid and the Saxone Shoe shop. Police are in attendance. The dining car is now preserved by the Railway Preservation Society of Ireland.

The new Headquarters of the UTA was at 21 Linenhall Street, a converted linen warehouse on the corner of Franklin Street. To the left is the back of the Ulster Hall. This shot was taken on 3 August 1949 (two days after the building opened) and shows a typical mix of cars. Left to right are a Hillman Minx, tail to tail with a 1938 Standard 'Flying Ten', beyond which appears a Vauxhall 'Big Six'. Facing away from the photographer on the other side of the road is a pre-war Ford Eight and on the corner of Franklin Street is a Post Office Morris Eight van.

This view of 21 Linenhall Street was taken from Franklin Street on 4 March 1950. A Vauxhall Velox is passing the front entrance.

The traffic lights at this junction were a novelty in 1950. Red was accompanied by the instruction 'Stop' and green by 'Go'!

In the foreground is a lovely 1939 Wolseley 18/85, a type popular with police forces in England and used by Inspector Foyle in the TV series *Foyle's War*. Passing in the opposite direction is a 1938 Austin Eighteen whilst parked on the left is a 1949 Riley RMA saloon.

On the buses

In 1951 the UTA purchased two luxury coaches built on the then new Leyland Royal Tiger chassis, intended for rail replacement services to Newcastle. The first of them was No E8931 (OZ 7966), which was also the first underfloor-engined bus bodied by the UTA. On 22 March 1951 the new coach was brought to the Malone Road for a photoshoot and two weeks later took senior staff for a run to the Slieve Donard Hotel, Newcastle, as seen opposite. These two coaches were finished in an Eau d'nil colour with dark green wheel arches and chrome trim.

An interior view of the new luxury coach at Newcastle on 5 April 1951. The coach had only 19 seats arranged 2+1, those on the offside being single seats. At the rear it had a toilet. Another interesting feature was that there were two tables with facing seats, one of which is occupied by three gentlemen in the photo. The man leaning out is thought to be Mr JA Clarke, then head of the UTA.

Apparently these vehicles were intended to be replacements for the saloon carriage used on the famous BCDR 'Golfers' Express' which took the Belfast élite to Newcastle on Saturday mornings. A card school operated on the train and this explains the two tables on the coaches!

The UTA quickly learned that rail passengers don't necessarily transfer to buses. Apparently the golfers didn't regard the new coaches as a suitable replacement for the train and just took their cars instead. The coaches were transferred to tour work and eventually reseated to 36 without tables or toilet.

For ordinary tours, the UTA provided much more spartan accommodation. Hotels like Fawcetts, Gastons and the Laharna operated tours of the province but had to depend on the UTA for the vehicles. As this photograph at Donegall Quay on Saturday 4 August 1951 shows, they got nothing better than a standard service bus. This was a constant grievance with both the NIRTB and the UTA who resolutely refused to buy proper coaches, of the standard common in England. Vehicles on Private Hire carried a 'P' rather than a route number. In the background, the left hand car is a 1948 Austin A40 Devon.

As if to disprove the point made opposite, here is a private hire vehicle not showing a 'P'! This view was taken at the RAC International Tourist Trophy Race, Dundrod, Co Antrim on 15 September 1951. Another view at this event is on the front cover. This was actually the first of the Dundrod races, which were discontinued after 1955 following a number of fatal accidents. A similar fate had befallen the Ards TT of 1928-36, which ended after eight spectators were killed in 1936. In Northern Ireland these car races were immensely popular and attracted big crowds. Today's Dundrod Races are motor cycle events. Bus No C8825 was one of 190 Leyland PS2/1 single deckers with larger engines, built at Dunmurry in 1948-49, following the 415 less powerful PS1s built in 1946-48. Most were later rebuilt as high bridge double-deckers.

Opposite the Smithfield Bus Station was a yard used by the UTA at North Street. This had originally been a bus depot used by the Belfast Omnibus Company (BOC), the largest of the pre-1935 private operators.

In the 1950s this was used by the UTA to store vehicles awaiting duties and to handle parcels traffic. Here, on 6 September 1951 an Inspector explains the duty to a conductor and driver about to take out one of the new Royal Tiger front entrance buses, then just entering service.

Note the 'Front Entrance' warning notice. Ulster passengers were so used to back door buses that, during the war, when some front entrance buses were requisitioned from England, a lady at Gibson Hill could not find the entrance and ran round to the offside before being rescued by the conductor!

The bus is now being loaded with parcels, some of which are being transferred from a parcel delivery van. From the rear, the Royal Tigers resembled a Leyland PS2 rear entrance bus. The parcels traffic was very lucrative as the overheads were low. A parcel delivered to North Street for, say, Cookstown would go on the next bus. A business simply phoned the customer to say "Your parcel is on the 10.15 bus." and it could be collected from the Cookstown depot by 1.15pm the same day.

The Festival Express

Partly as a relief to the austerity experienced in post-war Britain, the government decided to stage a 'Festival of Britain' in London on the centenary of the 1851 Great Exhibition. The UTA entered into the spirit of the celebrations by introducing a train named *The Festival* between Belfast and Londonderry. Official photographs of the new train were taken on the 'Back Loop', between Greenisland and Monkstown on 28 April 1951 with W class 2-6-0 No 100 *Queen Elizabeth* at the head.

On 3 May 1951, the first day of operation, the new train was photographed on arrival at York Road Station. Posing with the driver of No 99 *King George VI* are the UTA Secretary JA Clarke and Bill Hanley, the Locomotive Inspector on the railways.

The 'Queen Elizabeth' after whom No 100 was named was not the present Queen, who in 1951 was still Princess Elizabeth, but the wife of George VI, better known in our generation as the late Queen Mother.

This delightful photograph shows the cook on 'The Festival' at York Road Station on the same day as the previous picture. The Restaurant Car is No 87, previously seen on page 43 being delivered to York Road. The other carriages on the new train were from 16 new vehicles built at Duncrue Street in 1950-51. Often referred to as the 'Festival Stock', they were actually planned before the idea of the Festival Express had germinated. They were the last UTA carriages designed for steam trains and in the late 1950s were converted into Multi-Purpose Diesel railcars (MPDs).

One long-forgotten aspect of the UTA was the efforts of its publicity department to get children enthusiastic about transport. This is a Sand Designing Competition at Bangor on Saturday 5 August 1951. This contribution reads "Private tours every day are sent out by the UTA". I doubt if today's children could easily be recruited for such activity. What do you think Translink?

This shot, on 26 September 1949, is clearly posed as there is no house adjacent to explain the unloading! In the days of regulated road freight, the UTA was the first port of call if you were moving house. My own family moved twice using such vans, the first occasion being two months after this picture was taken. Some people moved house using private cars or vans with trailers but when it came to a paid professional service, the law permitted no competition to the UTA.

This is a delightful shot, taken on 12 September 1951 on the Hillhall Road. The reader might be forgiven for thinking it is a proposal of marriage, given the hand-holding and the coy looks. In fact the conductor on the No 13 bus is either accepting a parcel from the pretty young woman or delivering one to her. It is a reminder that rural buses offered this type of delivery service.

We also see detail of the entrance to the standard UTA 34 seat bus, with its three steps and folding doors.

The No 13 service ran from Belfast to Drumbo along the Hillhall Road, serving the Purdysburn Fever Hospital (now Belvoir) en route. The writer spent a year there in 1950-51 after contracting polio and his parents frequently used this service to visit him.

The famous 'Jerry trailer' featured prominently in the Festival of Britain Industrial Vehicles Parade in Belfast on 26 May 1951, with an industrial boiler as the load. This vehicle had come from Germany as part of post-war reparations. It is being hauled by Scammell Pioneer tractor No W3998, its year letter dating it to 1943. However, as its registration plate is 1948, this Scammell is probably a second-hand ex-army tank transporter. This view is in Donegall Square North as the parade passes the public under-street toilets in front of the City Hall. The amazing thing about this picture is the number of interested spectators. Today, probably most shoppers would probably ignore the parade and carry on with what they were doing.

The same parade featured this 1947 Commer 'Superpoise' flat bed lorry (GZ 5428) promoting the healthy attributes of Ryvita crispbread. The vehicle is seen passing the Bedford Agency on Bedford Street. Notice the twin sets of tram tracks. The square setts, once such a feature of city streets, were preferred to tarmac as the cobbles could be temporarily removed to repair the rails and were much harder wearing.

In 1951 the UTA placed a new experimental diesel train in service. It was made up of three vehicles converted from pre-war carriages and the end cars (Nos 6 and 7) were each powered by two 125hp AEC diesel engines. Car No 6 of the new train is seen here at York Road on 19 July 1951, just before it departed on a test run. The livery was UTA Brunswick green with a horizontal band in a light green between the windows and the cant rail. Following successful testing, the train went into service between Belfast and Bangor, though it was transferred back to the Larne line in 1953.

The three car train is seen switching tracks at Whitehead after the test run from Belfast. Members of the RPSI, whose headquarters is in located beyond the bridge, will be interested to see how the area to the right of the train looked in 1951. Despite the success of this AEC-powered train, when series production of the Multi-Engined Diesels (MEDs) began at Duncrue Street in 1952, the UTA used Leyland engines similar to the ones in their buses. This was fortunate as, when it was decided to fit more powerful 150hp engines in the trains in 1956, the earlier 125hp ones were easily recycled. Note the platform for unloading bread containers and the shelter for the bread man. The intermediate coach was No 279.

Going by Air

This is Glengall Street on 4 August 1951, looking towards Great Victoria Street, with the old Ulster Unionist headquarters on the left and the famous Grand Opera House visible above the bus. The passengers are outside the BEA Terminal and are transferring into one of three Leyland PS1 single-deckers which had five rear seats removed to create more luggage space and were painted into British European Airways red and cream. The 'Terminal' was a portacabin parked in Glengall Street close to the entrance of the present bus station. Note the absence of a nearside mirror on the bus. PSV regulations of the time did not permit one!

The buses were used to transfer passengers from Belfast to Nutt's Corner Aerodrome, seen here on 30 August 1951. In our age of airport security and lengthy check ins, we are used to elaborate terminal buildings with lounges and catering. Things were much simpler in 1951! You just walked over the tarmac from the aircraft to the bus. The airliner is a 'Pionair', more commonly known as a Dakota.

We end with a second view at Nutt's Corner Aerodrome. At the front of the aircraft is a Royal Mail van collecting mails, probably from London. The second bus is a standard UTA green 34 seater. During the war, Nutt's Corner had been a base for a Hurricane Squadron and it was to be 1963 before the airport was transferred to Aldergrove, where it eventually became Belfast International Airport. Over the years Nutt's Corner had been infested with hares which frequently played 'dare' with landing aircraft. Within a month of the move to nearby Aldergrove, hares appeared there too! The already established RAF swore there were no hares before the airliners arrived!